First published in the UK in 1989 by
Firefly Books Limited
61, Western Road, Hove
East Sussex BN3 1JD

British Library Cataloguing in Publication Data
Rosen, Michael, *1946–*
The tree: imagination
I. Title II. Series III. El árbol. *English*
823′.914 [J]
L.D.: B-26.562-89
ISBN 1 85485 003 2

Typeset by
Type Practitioners, Sevenoaks
Printed in Spain

Original title in Spanish: El Arbol – La Imaginación

Spanish text by Conxita Rodríguez
Illustrations by Conxita Rodríguez

Experiences

The Tree

IMAGINATION

Told by Michael Rosen

Illustration: Conxita Rodríguez

What is imagination?

You know when you wonder what you'll have for tea tonight and you start thinking of all the things you'd really like . . . that's your imagination working. You know when you wish you could be somebody brilliant and clever . . . that's your imagination working. And again, when you pretend you're somebody else, or somewhere else, that's imagination too. In fact, every time you start to say something that begins with: 'What if . . .', you're imagining things.

A tree at the end of the day. That's all. Simple as that. A tree, much like any other tree. The end of a day much like any other day. What could be more ordinary? But wait a minute! What's that in the tree. A monkey? Two monkeys? Let's get in a bit closer.

Ah no. Of course it's not monkeys. It's two boys. What would you like to call them? Alfredo? Wayne? Pablo? Darren? Well, the one who's upside down calls himself Crow and the one with the stripey T-shirt calls himself Biscuit. Crow comes from the big city far away while Biscuit lives here in the country. Every summer, Crow comes from the big city to stay with Biscuit, and every summer, they escape from the house and the village whenever they can to come to their special place – the tree.

And what a tree! If you stand next to the trunk, it feels like you're standing alongside a great brown giant. If you look up, it seems to climb and climb forever. Its branches and leaves make high-up dens and caves. So Crow and Biscuit follow their eyes and climb up. Then when they're up there, they can be astronauts floating past Venus, eagles perched on a cliff, or anything they want.

At the moment, as you can see, they're on board a raft, lost in the middle of the Atlantic Ocean. 'I can see something in the water,' shouts Crow.

'It's a bottle,' says Crow, 'I'll go for it.'

'No don't, Crow, don't. If you fall in, our raft will drift on and you'll drown.'

'But it's a bottle. It might have a message in it.'

'What good is some old bottle?' said Biscuit. 'A bottle can't save us, can it?'

'Hold on to me,' said Crow, 'I'm going for it.'

'No, stop it, Crow, you're going to fall out of the tree. It's not a bottle. It's just your lunch box.'

They climbed down. Biscuit picked up his remote control car:

'I'm starving,' he said.

'Listen,' said Crow, 'tomorrow when we come back, we'll climb the cliffs to the baron's castle, sneak into the cellars and steal the treasure.'

'What are you talking about?' said Biscuit.

'The tree, the tree,' said Crow.

'Oh yes,' said Biscuit.

That night, the boys were dozing off when Crow suddenly sat up.

'Stand back, Baron. We know where the treasure is. And we know where it comes from. You stole this treasure from the king and we have come to take it back to him. Aah – I've been seized. I didn't see that guard behind the door. Sir Biscuit, they're taking us to the dungeons.'

'Are they?' said Biscuit, 'oh dear.'

'Crow?' said Biscuit.
'Mmm?' said Crow.
'It is only a tree, isn't it?' said Biscuit.
'Sure it is,' said Crow and dozed off.

Biscuit was floating in his sleep.

'I can fly too,' he said to the birds.

'Not as high as us,' said the birds.

'But I can fly too,' said Biscuit.

'Not as fast as us,' said the birds.

'But I can fly too,' said Biscuit.

'Not as far as us,' said the birds.

'Not as far as us . . . not as far as us . . . not as far as us.'

'This could be dangerous,' said Crow the next day as they ran through the woods.

'Why?' said Biscuit.

'Tigers – look!'

'But that's only Dusty. Here Dusty, here boy!'

'It's a tiger, young man, believe me. Quick we must escape. Follow me.'

'Don't run so fast, Crow.'

'Quick, into this balloon, we only have twenty seconds before the tiger eats us up.'

'I can't climb trees as fast as you, Crow.'

'Let go of the rope, and we're away,' shouted Crow.

'Run home, Dusty,' said Biscuit.

'Man-eating tiger that, you know,' said Crow.

'Look, Biscuit, that's the coast of France.'

'Is it?' said Biscuit.

'And there's Paris,' said Crow.

'Look, there's the Eiffel Tower,' said Biscuit.

‘What are you drawing?’ said Biscuit.

‘Our tree,’ said Crow.

‘It doesn’t look much like a tree,’ said Biscuit, ‘looks more like some kind of poster . . . air balloon, spaceship, castle, raft . . . where’s the tree?’

‘There,’ said Crow, ‘you’re looking at it. Listen, a tree with branches and leaves is just what everyone else says is a tree. Our tree is a castle, a spaceship and all these things. I’ll show this picture to my friends when I get home.’

‘Oh yes,’ said Biscuit, ‘I’d forgotten. You’re going back to the big city tomorrow, aren’t you?’

‘Mmm,’ said Crow, ‘that’s right. I’ve got to get back to tell the newspapers about the man-eating tiger.’

‘Oh yes,’ said Biscuit, ‘but hang on, what tiger?’